GET YOUR WAR ON II

GET YOUR WAR ON II

DAVID REES

RIVERHEAD BOOKS
NEW YORK

Riverhead Books
Published by The Berkley Publishing Group
A division of Penguin Group (USA) Inc.
375 Hudson Street
New York, New York 10014

GET YOUR WAR ON II

Many of the strips in this book have appeared in *Rolling Stone, Punk Planet,* and online. Strips dated with an asterisk have been changed since their original appearance.

First Riverhead trade paperback edition: September 2004
Riverhead trade paperback ISBN: 1-59448-048-6

This book has been catalogued with the Library of Congress.

Printed in the United States of America

10   9   8   7   6   5   4   3   2   1

For Lt. General William G. "Jerry" Boykin and Senator James H. Inhofe, a couple of goddamn idiots.

AUTHOR'S NOTE: I recently uncovered these classic *Get Your War On* cartoons in my attic. I made them in the 1980s, when I was young and naive. The drawing, grammar, and typography of these early strips are a little crude, but I believe they offer valuable context for today's foreign policy issues.

September 27, 2002

September 27, 2002

September 27, 2002

September 27, 2002

September 27, 2002

November 5, 2002

November 26, 2002

November 26, 2002

November 26, 2002

November 26, 2002

November 26, 2002

January 4, 1861

May 11, 1863

January 15, 2003*

January 19, 2003

January 19, 2003

January 19, 2003

January 19, 2003

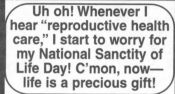

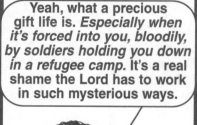

January 19, 2003 *

January 19, 2003

*January 19, 2003**

January 29, 2003

February 10, 2003

February 10, 2003

February 10, 2003

February 10, 2003

February 10, 2003

Jesus, this UK dossier on Iraq's concealment infrastructure is a total fuckin' hodge-podge! Can someone say, "C-"? Did they order the thing out of the back of *Tiger Beat*?

People are gonna go *die* because of this document. Could you at least reword the passages you TOTALLY COPIED from outdated sources? Or get someone other than a spotty Manchester United-jersey-wearin' intern to handle the important paragraphs? For fuck's sake! Their concealment infrastructure dossiers are as crappy as their "news"-papers! (Thanks for being our "girlfriend" though, Mr. Blair!)

OH MY GOD!!! I just remembered! Saddam gassed his own people!!!

Beep beep!

February 10, 2003

February 14, 2003

February 26, 2003

February 14, 2003

March 10, 2003

March 10, 2003

March 10, 2003

March 10, 2003

March 10, 2003

March 10, 2003

March 20, 2003

March 20, 2003

March 20, 2003

March 20, 2003

March 20, 2003

Just promise me one thing. Promise me that when you hear Saddam Hussein is dead, you'll stop moaning about this war for a moment and think of all the people that odious motherfucker killed. Raise a glass to his victims.

You know what? Don't give me that shit. *I know when to grieve, and who for.* Those sanctions made Saddam stronger and his victims weaker. Yet, somehow, *mentioning this fact to people over the years* made me a "hippie." A HIPPIE? I'm a middle manager who lifts weights and doesn't like the smell of marijuana! Meanwhile, Donald Rumsfeld is about to be treated as a humanitarian liberator! You don't need to tell me who to "raise a glass to," you fucking idiot—I raise six glasses every night, just to get drunk enough to love this country like I did as a kid: without feeling like it's *using me.*

Come on, I was trying to have a moment!

March 20, 2003

March 20, 2003

April 9, 2003

March 26, 2003*

April 9, 2003

April 9, 2003

April 9, 2003

April 9, 2003

April 9, 2003

April 9, 2003

April 9, 2003

April 9, 2003

I was on a self-imposed international news embargo for the past week. Lemme ask you, man—is George W. Bush's foreign policy actually *working?*

If by *"working"* you mean *"ratcheting up every international relationship to pants-shitting intensity,"* then the answer is "yes." I think future scholars will refer to it as the *"Grand Theft Auto* School of Diplomacy."

Remember *Q*bert?* Where all you did was fuckin' hop up and down the steps all day? God, I loved that game. I never *woke up screaming* after playing it, that's for damn sure!

April 24, 2003

OK, I'm finally ready to issue my personal press statement about SARS: "(*Ahem*) THANKS FOR TRYING TO KILL THE WORLD, CHINA!"

Here's my statement about Bush's bodilicious landing on the USS *Abraham Lincoln*, when he could have just fuckin' swum out to it: "HELL, I DIDN'T WANT TO SERVE IN VIETNAM, EITHER. DOES THAT MEAN I CAN FLY IN A VIKING JET SOMEDAY?"

Would you like to hear my statement about the increase in American black children living in extreme poverty? It has to do with a rising tide lifting all boats, except the boats nobody gives a fuck about. Here goes: "YOUR BALLS MUST BE BRASSIER THAN HERB ALPERT TO DEMAND AN ENORMOUS TAX CUT RIGHT—"

Oh, God, if they don't find some serious weapons of mass destruction in Iraq, I'm gonna feel SO used!

May 7, 2003

The GYWO Players in:
"Have You Seen My Book of Virtues?"

May 8, 2003

May 8, 2003

Hi, Merrill Lynch? I'm calling about my missing Book of Virtues. I wondered if you had it. Yes, I'll hold.

At some point during the course of gambling away eight million dollars, do you at least *consider* donating the money to, like, a drug abuse clinic instead? Or are the stakes at those places not high enough? Though maybe that would be just be SO UNREASONABLY MORAL that it would put you over the edge, and your fuckin' *head would explode* with all the prolapsed goodness!

You know what I like about you, Merrill Lynch? You really do your best to keep the heads-exploding-with-goodness to an absolute minimum. *Sure, I'll continue to hold!*

May 8, 2003

May 8, 2003

May 8, 2003

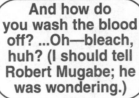

May 8, 2003

May 8, 2003

May 8, 2003

May 21, 2003

Why aren't you at work? You think just because Ari Fleischer, Christie Whitman, and Tommy Franks are calling it quits, you can too?

Whoa—*what if the three of them quit because they're starting a band together?* Talk about a—

I got laid off. I'm standing in my kitchen wearing *pleated shorts!* And, by God, if we haven't invaded Iran by the time my checking account balance hits zero, there's gonna be a problem.

May 30, 2003*

Keep your chin up. Remember what Jay Garner said before he was dethroned as Pretend-King of Iraq: "*We ought to be beating our chests every day. We ought to look in a mirror and be proud, and stick out our chests and suck in our bellies, and say: Damn, we're Americans!*"

May 30, 2003*

Yeah, it's real easy to look in a mirror and be proud when you're wearing pleated shorts. And you know what's really pathetic? I don't even have any dividends to get tax-decreased. When'll they cut taxes on not-having-health-insurancends?

Don't worry—I'm such a loser I don't know what a dividend *is*. When they start cutting taxes on shit I can't even *define*, I know it's time to start buying condensed milk. *Goddamn lumpy-ass milk.*

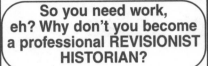

May 30, 2003

The GYWO Players in:
"Cavalcade of Knock-Knock Jokes"

June 5, 2003

June 5, 2003

June 5, 2003

June 5, 2003

June 5, 2003

Vroom, vroom! Outta my way! I've got the pedal to the metal, driving the ROAD MAP TO PEACE! *Honk, honk!* Israeli settlers, time to pull up stakes and move the fuck out! Palestinian suicide bombers, time to keep your goddamn explosions to yourselves!

I'm so glad that Pat Robertson is sharing his views on the road map with Washington: "*If they do anything other than make Jerusalem the capital of Israel, they would be messing with the word and the power of God.*" Hey, Pat, is 9/11 still the fault of atheists and lesbians, you fucking INSANE RELIGIOUS PRICK? Why is this guy allowed to weigh in on *anything*? (PS: "*Messing*"? What, are we poking God with a stick?)

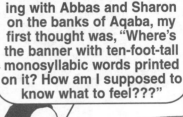

When I saw Bush standing with Abbas and Sharon on the banks of Aqaba, my first thought was, "Where's the banner with ten-foot-tall monosyllabic words printed on it? How am I supposed to know what to feel???"

Seriously, though: Good luck, everyone!

June 5, 2003

July 2, 2003

July 17, 2003

July 30, 2003

August 11, 2003

"Killing You is a Very Easy Thing For Us": Human Rights Abuses in Southeast Afghanistan
Human Rights Watch, 2003

August 12, 2003

August 19, 2003

August 19, 2003*

August 19, 2003

August 19, 2003

August 19, 2003

August 19, 2003

August 19, 2003

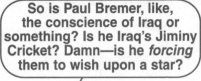

August 19, 2003

I can't believe it's already been two years. I'm so exhausted—I feel like I started running a marathon on September 12th, 2001, and I haven't stopped since. *And I'm fucking sick of it.* I'm sick of feeling like I gotta read the newspaper every day. I'm sick of having to open my atlas every goddamn time there's a new terror threat. I'm sick of President Bush acting like half our allies in the war on terrorism aren't total fucking creeps. I'm sick of Donald Rumsfeld's gray skin and naked contempt. I'm sick of feeling queasy every time I go to the gas station. I'm sick of trying to remain optimistic. I'm sick of hearing about refugees and kids with no fucking arms. I'm sick of left-wingers and right-wingers slinging shit and trying to *out-patriot* each other. I'm sick of Lower Manhattan's skyline looking like... *Decatur*, or some fucking two-bit wannabe metropolis. And I'm sick of all the tattered, fading flags—buy a new fucking flag if you're such a patriot, for fuck's sake! I'm sick of my friends being unemployed. I'm sick of my kids asking me when the world will be better. I'm sick of not trusting anybody with a microphone. I'm *truly* sick of dumb motherfuckers who think Saddam Hussein had something to do with it. I'm sick of think tanks. Fucking stupid think thanks—would you stop thinking and fucking *fix something*, for fuck's sake? I'm sick of people who argue with me. I'm sick of worrying if I've been wrong all along. I'm sick of people writing speeches for children and giving them to adults. I'm sick of Joe Lieberman. Please, *please* shut up, Joe Lieberman. I'm sick of sirens. I'm sick of the smell of alcohol. I'm sick of crying when I hear *Rhapsody in Blue*. I'm sick of feeling empty.

You know what I'm sick of? I'm sick of my cousin being dead.

August 19, 2003 (September 11, 2003)

September 15, 2003

October 1, 2003

I work for *New Bridge Strategies*, identifying market opportunities in Iraq! I also know George W. Bush! *Gee, I wonder if I'm about to make a shitload of money?*

So if my company wants to make money in postwar Iraq, I call you guys, right? Any idealistic hippies over there at New Bridge Strategies?

Huh? Sorry, I was fantasizing about privatizing Iraq's water supply! [*Blush*] And now I have a "Stiff Bridge Strategy" in my pants! *Dude, I'm really psyched to vote for Howard Dean—NOT!*

I heard one of your partners boast, "One well-stocked 7-Eleven could knock out thirty Iraqi stores!" Remind me why we hate Iraqi stores, again? No Slurpees?

Hooray, California! You're winning the Stupid contest!

"The Lefty's Lament"

Why am I such a fuck-up? Why did I forget to make money in postwar Iraq?

October 8, 2003

October 16, 2003

October 20, 2003

October 28, 2003

October 21, 2003

Panel 1: If Bush loses the election, will Dick Cheney and Donald Rumsfeld go back on welfare?

Panel 2: Yeah—they'll go back to being *real* poor. They'll probably have to choose between paying their credit card bills and paying their health insurance.

Panel 3: You know, sometimes I wonder—everyone in the White House is so much richer than the people they rule, it's kind of sad. How much richer would they have to be before it became *funny*?

Panel 4: *Later...* I figured it out: They'd each have to make eleven dollars more per year! PS: Did you know we just engaged in *CLASS WARFARE*???

November 6, 2003

Do you feel safer now that Saddam Hussein has been over-thrown?

Actually, you know what makes me feel *real* safe? Knowing that Donald Rumsfeld and Dick Cheney can get anything they want, no matter what. Even a war. That's *bad-ass*.

I've never gotten a single war I wanted!

We can put a man on the moon; we can make the biggest damn cars in the world; and we can invade countries for mythical reasons. America dwells in the Age of Wizardry.

Excelsior!

Later...

I thought of another cool thing about America in the Age of Wizardry: When our soldiers die, they turn invisible. I used to think only Iraqi civilians had that power!

November 6, 2003

I was feeling depressed about a certain ~~quagmire~~ challenge, so I went to Virginia for the Iraq Infrastructure Reconstruction Office's conference for prospective bidders.

Ooh, I was there! I'm gonna bid on mailing out America's Christmas card to Iraq! It says, *"Season's Greetings/We always hated supporting Saddam/Did you hate getting killed by him?/ FEEL GRATEFUL, GODDAMMIT/Peace on Earth."* It has a frowning Christmas tree on the front.

At the conference, Congressman Tom Davis* said rebuilding Iraq was our duty and that "if you make noble sacrifices along the way, all the better." No, sorry—Nonexistent Man said that. Davis said, "If you *make a profit* along the way, all the better." So can I make a profit building a "Tackiest Asshole" award for Tom Davis?

*(R, Virginia.) *Thank you, Virginia. You may go now.*

November 20, 2003

December 8, 2003

December 9, 2003

And of course that f---er Andy Card says he's "very disappointed Kerry would use that kind of language." GIVE ME A F---ING BREAK!!!

December 9, 2003

Who elected Andy Card head schoolmarm of the United States? Hey, Andy Card—you wanna do something that's actually f---ing useful? Ask your f---ing boss to fix the tremendous f----up he's created in Iraq by f---ing firing that insane motherf---er Donald Rumsfeld!

Donald Rumsfeld. Now *there's* someone who doesn't have a limited vocabulary.

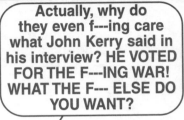

December 9, 2003

December 9, 2003

December 9, 2003

December 9, 2003

December 9, 2003

December 9, 2003

December 9, 2003

December 9, 2003

December 14, 2003

December 15, 2003

December 23, 2003

December 31, 2003

January 6, 2004

January 7, 2004

January 14, 2004

January 14, 2004

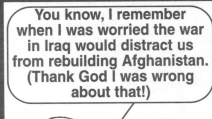

January 14, 2004

January 14, 2004

January 14, 2004

January 14, 2004

January 14, 2004

January 22, 2004

January 22, 2004

I have mixed feelings about invading Iraq. I'm a little glad we did it, but I'm also relieved to know I wasn't an idiot FOR FEELING TOTALLY SAFE FROM SADDAM HUSSEIN for the past twenty years.

January 22, 2004

What about the "dozens of weapons of mass destruction-related program activities" we've found in Iraq?

You see, when the situation can only be described by a phrase *that's so fuckin' long I can hardly remember how to say it correctly*, I kind of give up feeling scared.

January 22, 2004

January 22, 2004*

January 30, 2004

February 9, 2004

February 12, 2004

February 16, 2004

February 23, 2004

February 27, 2004

March 8, 2004

March 2, 2004*

March 9, 2004

March 11, 2004

March 11, 2004

March 23, 2004

March 23, 2004

March 23, 2004

March 24, 2004

April 1, 2004

April 1, 2004

April 1, 2004

April 8, 2004

April 16, 2004

OK, really. What am I supposed to say? "Thank you, President Bush, for holding a prime-time press conference? Your crumbs are so delicious? It means so much to us that you took precious time away from your stupid fuckin' hole-in-the-wall, dusty backasswards fake-ass ranch down in dipshit CRAWFORD, TEXAS to speak to us about the crappy war in Iraq that you and your staff completely fucked up because you're a bunch of FUCKING EGOMANIACAL RETARDS?"

No you DIDN'T! No you didn't make fun of the ranch in Crawford, Texas! Typical East Coast elitist!

"East Coast elitist?" Fuck it, sure—is that what you call it? Fine. All I know is I'm from New York City, I can think on my feet, I can actually *string two fuckin' sentences together* without notes, and I could answer some motherfuckers' questions *about a war* without just spitting out eleven different permutations of the same goddamn "*goo-gah boogaloo freedom*" phrase! So sue me—that makes me elitist? Good! If "*elitist*" just means "*not the dumbest motherfucker in the room*," I'll be an elitist!

April 16, 2004

Look, if President Bush had whatever Stephen Hawking has, and he couldn't speak correctly because his face was all frozen up and drooly and he rolled around D.C. in a motorized wheelchair with Condoleezza Rice feeding him oatmeal—then I wouldn't care how he talked. But the dude is like, the MOST PHYSICALLY FIT MAN IN AMERICA. He went to YALE. What the fuck?

You think just because the words are garbled in his mouth, they're garbled in his mind?

Hell yes they're garbled in his mind! His mind is like one of those spinning cages where you pull out the winning lottery numbers—but there's only four fuckin' little balls in his cage: "Freedom," "Democracy," "Terror," and "Stay the Course." He opens his mouth, one of the balls drops out. That's not a conversation, that's Keno.

Wait—who said anything about having a conversation?

April 16, 2004

You know what's weird? It's almost like, when we moved troops from Afghanistan to Iraq, we moved all our Stay the Course and Stand Our Ground too. I don't think we left a single Stay the Course lying around over there.

You know what the bottom line is? If Bush was a doctor he'd use the "get well soon" card to diagnose the illness.

Are you suggesting that if we're fighting a "war of ideas" in the Muslim world, we need a commander-in-chief who can successfully *express one* when he opens his mouth? I always thought the White House was just handicapping itself so the Clash of Civilizations wouldn't look fixed.

April 16, 2004

Complicated times call for simple language! How else do you justify being allies with Pakistan without *your head exploding from cognitive dissonance?*

Listen. Me *like* simple words. Make me feel STRONG, like "Hulk *SMASH!*" But simple words plus geopolitical strategy contingent on morally compromised transnational alliances not so great. Maybe? Or me bad citizen for think that?

Listen, man— What part of "Freedom Freedom Stay the Course Terror Terror" don't you understand?

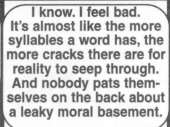

I know. I feel bad. It's almost like the more syllables a word has, the more cracks there are for reality to seep through. And nobody pats themselves on the back about a leaky moral basement.

April 16, 2004*

April 16, 2004

April 16, 2004

Apologies to B. Breathed

April 16, 2004

April 16, 2004

April 22, 2004

Remind me why some people think Bush is tough? Because he walks around with his arms sticking out from his sides like an inflatable man? "You know how we do things in Crawford, Texas? When we have to answer tough questions, we get our Vice President to come along so he can *hold our hand like a goddamn baby.*"

Seriously, though? I would've asked Richard Perle to hold my hand. His hands look *so* soft.

That's because he's never had to wring them together, *because he's never been wrong.*

Is Crawford, Texas secretly the touchy-feely capital of the world? If I ask a Crawford mechanic why he let my engine get fucked up, will the other guys in the garage be sitting there holding his hands the whole time?

April 29, 2004

May 6, 2004

May 6, 2004

May 13, 2004

May 15, 2004

May 15, 2004

May 15, 2004*

May 24, 2004

You know what thought woke me up at three in the morning last night? Rumsfeld, Feith, and Perle are actually *more incompetent than they are evil.* How the hell is that possible?

You know what I realized? All these guys you see on TV, speaking about Iraq and sovereignty and June 30th and whatnot? *None of them has any fucking idea what they're talking about.* I listened to those blowhards for over a year and I didn't learn A SINGLE GODDAMN CORRECT THING. They talk out of their asses so much *their cushions are probably deaf.* I'd learn more about the future of Iraq if I read a Golden Book Encyclopedia upside-down in the dark.

Ooh—if you do that, will you look up the entry for "ignore"? I want to know if it still has that picture of Sudan.

May 27, 2004

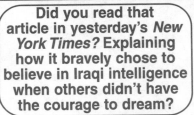

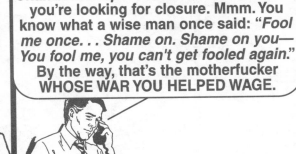

May 27, 2004

Fuck a mild-mannered apology on Page 10. The only honest way for the *New York Times* to deal with this shit would have been to run a big-ass banner headline that says, "WHY THE HELL ARE YOU STILL READING US? DOES JUDITH MILLER HAVE TO KILL YOU HERSELF?"

May 27, 2004

What about, "All the news that's fit to print, if by '*fit to print*' you mean '*un-fact-checkable horseshit pulled out of some con-man's ass and solemnly regurgitated on the front page, just so we could keep sitting at the tough guys table*'?"

And you know what's most embar-rassing for the *Times*? They probably forgot to charge Chalabi a promotional fee.

May 27, 2004

The closer we move to June 30th, the more excited I get! Has Iraq decided who's gonna land the jet of sovereignty on their aircraft carrier of destiny? Sovereignty *rocks!* (What is it, by the way?)

"Sovereignty." Parsed much? As of this evening, it means Iraqis will finally take control of Iraq.

Wow. With all the shit they've been through over the years, we couldn't find them a nicer country to take control of than *Iraq*?

May 27, 2004

May 27, 2004*

May 27, 2004*

"GOOD OL' UZBEKIKITTY! CAN'T WAIT TO SEE THE GARFIELD MOVIE!"

Meow! People are complaining about how I treated one of my prisoners!

"Shelkavenko had an open, bloody head wound approximately 5 centimeters long on the left side of his scalp, along with abrasion and indentation on the right side of his neck, and a long wound to the back of his neck. He also had bruises on the underside of his right arm, and abrasions on the back of his shoulders. (His) scrotum was unevenly blackened and swollen, and he had a long indentation at the top of his left thigh. He had a bloody wound on his right leg and scratches on the backs of his ankles."

Can you top *that*, Amerikitty?

Uzbekistan: New Torture Death Belies Claims of Progress
Human Rights Watch, 2004

May 27, 2004

June 3, 2004*

June 28, 2004

June 28, 2004

June 28, 2004

June 28, 2004

June 28, 2004

July 1, 2004

July 6, 2004

Is Operation Iraqi Freedom the most expensive botched American thing ever?

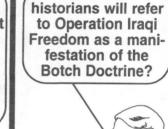

The only thing that could've been more botched would be if in 1969 America had landed on the moon using a rocket that only flew one way—with a crew of 130,000 astronauts who then killed 10,000 moon men. We botched this motherfucker like botching was going out of style. This thing was so fuckin' botched, I'm surprised the name of the war wasn't misspelled.

I wonder if historians will refer to Operation Iraqi Freedom as a manifestation of the Botch Doctrine?

July 6, 2004

People who complain about the botched occupation seem to have forgotten one thing—*Donald Rumsfeld's military push towards Baghdad was brilliant.*

Yeah right! Maybe I missed something, but wasn't the "military push" basically just us driving through the desert? That's "brilliant?" *Driving in a straight line to get somewhere?* And as far as defeating Saddam's army. . . look, no disrespect, but the goddamn *NBA* could have defeated Saddam's army. Big fuckin' deal—what was it, like a thousand malnourished motherfuckers in khakis shooting rifles from 1980? I bet the black market price for white flags quadrupled in Iraq last spring. And our military thought *that* was the fight to win? Um, that wasn't the fight to win, you strategic masterminds.

There's a new law at the Army War College: *Any fight with Ted Koppel riding in a tank is automatically not that important.*

July 6, 2004

July 6, 2004

July 6, 2004

July 6, 2004

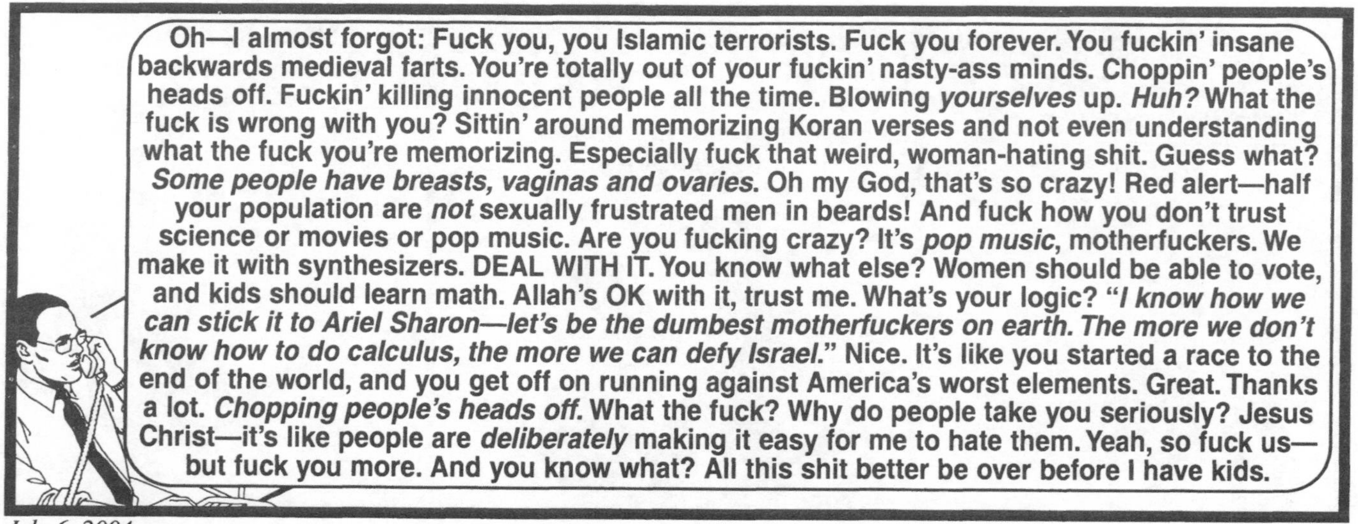
Oh—I almost forgot: Fuck you, you Islamic terrorists. Fuck you forever. You fuckin' insane backwards medieval farts. You're totally out of your fuckin' nasty-ass minds. Choppin' people's heads off. Fuckin' killing innocent people all the time. Blowing *yourselves* up. *Huh?* What the fuck is wrong with you? Sittin' around memorizing Koran verses and not even understanding what the fuck you're memorizing. Especially fuck that weird, woman-hating shit. Guess what? *Some people have breasts, vaginas and ovaries.* Oh my God, that's so crazy! Red alert—half your population are *not* sexually frustrated men in beards! And fuck how you don't trust science or movies or pop music. Are you fucking crazy? It's *pop music*, motherfuckers. We make it with synthesizers. DEAL WITH IT. You know what else? Women should be able to vote, and kids should learn math. Allah's OK with it, trust me. What's your logic? "*I know how we can stick it to Ariel Sharon—let's be the dumbest motherfuckers on earth. The more we don't know how to do calculus, the more we can defy Israel.*" Nice. It's like you started a race to the end of the world, and you get off on running against America's worst elements. Great. Thanks a lot. *Chopping people's heads off.* What the fuck? Why do people take you seriously? Jesus Christ—it's like people are *deliberately* making it easy for me to hate them. Yeah, so fuck us—but fuck you more. And you know what? All this shit better be over before I have kids.

July 6, 2004

July 6, 2004

What is the Global Landmine Crisis?

Long after peace treaties are signed and armies have returned home, landmines continue to kill and maim thousands of people every year, and prevent the productive use of land. In fact, the global landmine crisis is one of the world's most pervasive problems, with an estimated 70 countries considered to be mine-affected.

- A minefield is an area suspected of containing mines— an area that is rendered uninhabitable or that cannot be cultivated or put to productive use because local populations fear entering into it.
- Tragically, fundamental human instincts and the need for food often compel adults and children alike to enter mined areas.
- Landmines are designed to target civilian populations, disrupt people's lives, and displace entire communities from their homes and agricultural bases.
- Estimated landmines worldwide: 45 to 70 million.
- Cost of producing a landmine: as little as $3.
- Cost of removing a landmine: up to $1,000.
- Annual reported landmine accidents: 15,000 to 20,000
- Over 70% of these victims are civilians; many are children.

If landmines are present or even thought to be present, community members can face economic loss, an inability to access water and food sources, and treacherous transportation routes. These indiscriminate weapons of war threaten the daily life of hundreds of thousands of people; endanger children, returning refugees and livestock; and pollute the environment.

Adopt-A-Minefield

In response to the global landmine crisis, the Adopt-A-Minefield (AAM) Campaign was created by the United Nations Association of the USA in partnership with the United Nations, Ted Turner's Better World Fund, and the U.S. State Department to clear minefields, provide assistance to landmine survivors, and raise awareness of the global landmine crisis.

Since its launch in 1999, AAM has quickly become one of the world's leading mine clearance programs. It is the only nongovernmental funder in the top donor list in six of the most heavily mined countries in the world: Afghanistan, Bosnia and Herzegovina, Cambodia, Croatia, Mozambique, and Vietnam.

The idea behind AAM is simple, yet powerful. Designed to move beyond the political and policy debates typically associated with banning the use of landmines, the Campaign provides a practical solution to ridding the world of mines. The Campaign seeks national and international sponsors to adopt minefields; to adopt 2-month work periods for demining teams; or donate funds for survivor assistance projects.

If you'd like to donate to AAM, please make out a check to Adopt-A-Minefield and send to:

Adopt-A-Minefield
United Nations Association of the USA
801 Second Avenue
New York, NY 10017-4706
www.landmines.org